# Miss You to Pieces

## A Deployment Story and Project Idea for Kids

*Written by*
## Donna M. Purkey

*Illustrated by*
## Beth Wehner and Emily M. Erbig

This book is dedicated to my children,
Ryan and Leann,
who inspire me and make me laugh every day.

ISBN: 1470158035
ISBN-13: 9781470158033
Library of Congress Control Number: 2012903847
CreateSpace, North Charleston, SC

# Author's Note

Thank you for purchasing this book. I hope it inspires you to be creative and optimistic; and that it will be a source of comfort and encouragement to you and your children.

There is no doubt that our military family lifestyle can be stressful and challenging; and deployments are especially hard to explain to our children. While older children are more capable of experiencing pride and patriotism, younger children often experience a wider range of negative emotions (including sadness, anger, fear, loneliness, abandonment, anxiety and guilt) during deployment. These feelings can be both scary and overwhelming to them. Having positive strategies for coping with these emotions can make an enormous difference for them, and for us.

As a Navy wife and the mother of two young children, I have learned that being prepared isn't always enough; and that a positive attitude can be a tremendous asset. Being creative helps too! When my children were very young and needed visuals to understand the concept of time, we made the traditional paper chain when my husband deployed. The length of it was depressing and tearing off a link each day had no real meaning for my children. Plus, counting <u>backwards</u> was inconceivable to them at the time.

That's when I decided to count UP the days of the deployment, and in doing so, teach my children to count past 100. It made much more sense to add pieces to a project, to build something, and to have something to show Dad when he got home. And so, the puzzle project idea was born. It gave us a more meaningful and positive way to count the days, and provided us with an opportunity each day to chat with each other and connect. My children were so eager to work on their puzzles every night, and so proud to show others what they had accomplished. The puzzles they have completed are framed and have become treasured keepsakes in our home.

I encourage you to create your own puzzle project to provide a positive coping strategy for your children. You will simultaneously foster their emotional development and strengthen their bond with you, and their deployed parent.

Finally, the puzzle project is not limited to military families. It can, and should, be adapted to accommodate ANY family's separation whether it is for a parent traveling for work or counting the days until grandparents come to visit.

Stay connected ~ just like your puzzle pieces!

Please read *Tips for Your Puzzle Project* at the end of the book.

Hi! My name is Riley and I'm part of a really cool family! I love to do fun things with my mom and dad like ride bikes, go camping, and play games. Being together as a family is one of my favorite things in the world, but it doesn't happen every day. That's because my dad is a sailor in the United States Navy.

He works on a ship that goes out in the ocean. Most of the time it's just for a few days, but sometimes he goes away for a long time, and I really miss him. It's hard to be apart, which is why I felt so sad when my dad told me about a big trip he was going on.

"I'm going to be away for six months," he said. "I know that's a pretty long time, but Mom has a lot of fun things planned for you to do."

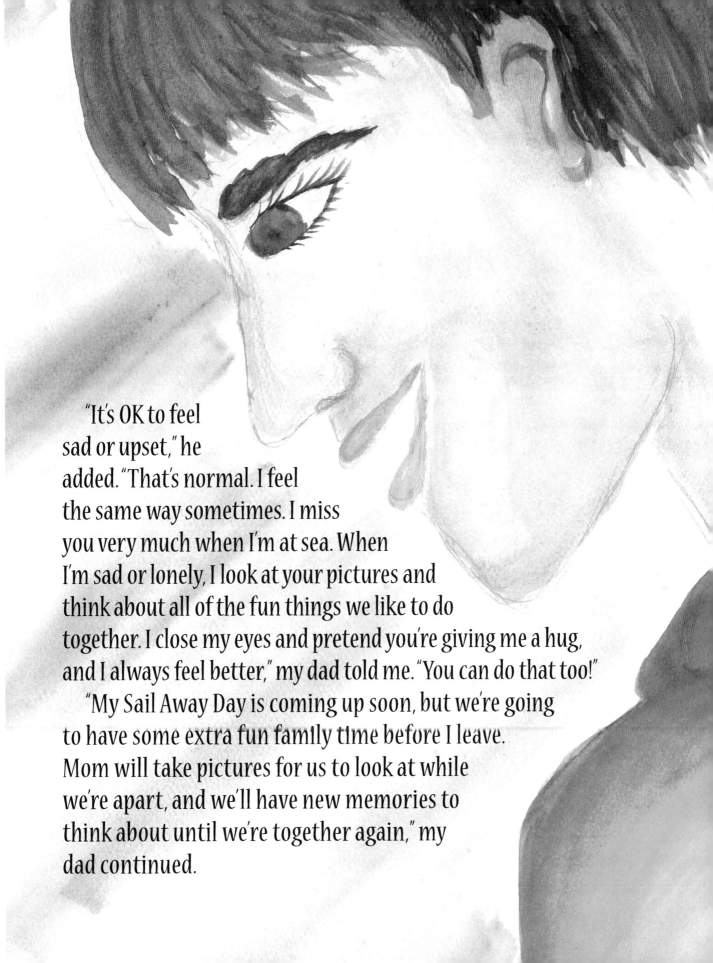

"It's OK to feel
sad or upset," he
added. "That's normal. I feel
the same way sometimes. I miss
you very much when I'm at sea. When
I'm sad or lonely, I look at your pictures and
think about all of the fun things we like to do
together. I close my eyes and pretend you're giving me a hug,
and I always feel better," my dad told me. "You can do that too!"

"My Sail Away Day is coming up soon, but we're going
to have some extra fun family time before I leave.
Mom will take pictures for us to look at while
we're apart, and we'll have new memories to
think about until we're together again," my
dad continued.

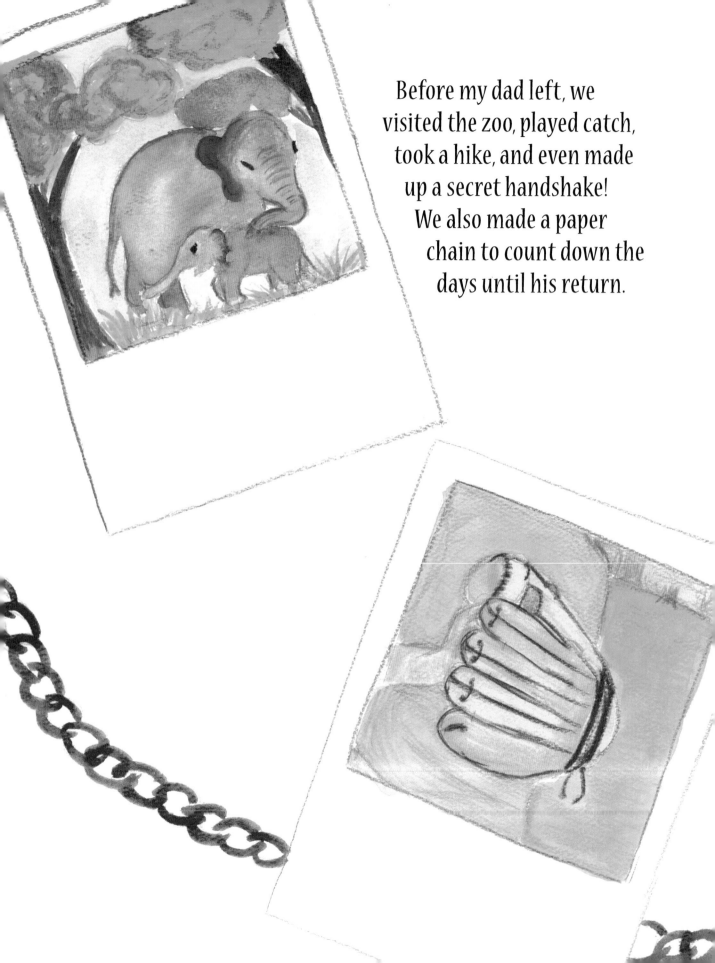

Before my dad left, we visited the zoo, played catch, took a hike, and even made up a secret handshake! We also made a paper chain to count down the days until his return.

The chain was super long! We hung it in my room so each day I could tear off a link and see how much longer we had to wait.

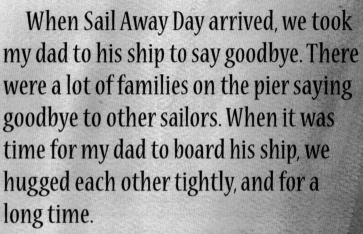

When Sail Away Day arrived, we took my dad to his ship to say goodbye. There were a lot of families on the pier saying goodbye to other sailors. When it was time for my dad to board his ship, we hugged each other tightly, and for a long time.

"I love you, Riley," my dad said. "I'll miss you, but I'll be thinking about you all the time; and I'll call you every chance I get. Be good for Mom and give her lots of extra hugs."

"I love you too, Dad," I answered quietly. I had a weird feeling in my stomach. I knew he had to go, but I *really* just wanted him to stay.

"How about one more secret handshake?" my dad suggested. As we shook hands in our own secret way, I felt a smile on my face, and thought, *maybe things won't be so bad.*

We all hugged one last time, and then my dad
left. It was hard to watch him go. My mom and I
waited on the pier while the ship sailed away. We
waved and waved until it was out of sight. My
mom cried a little, and so did I.

Then, my mom hugged me and said, "Don't worry, Riley. Everything is going to be okay. We have a lot to look forward to and we'll be busy, so the time will go by fast. Plus, I have a few surprises for you while Dad's away."

"Really? What kind of surprises?" I asked.

"Come on, let's go. I'll show you!" she exclaimed.

When we got home, my mom gave me a box of puzzle pieces.
"What's this?" I asked.
"Your first surprise. It's a special puzzle project!" my mom
replied. "You have to put the pieces together in a certain order, so
I've numbered the backs for you to know which piece to add next.
You can add one piece each day, and when it's done, Dad will be
home!" she explained.

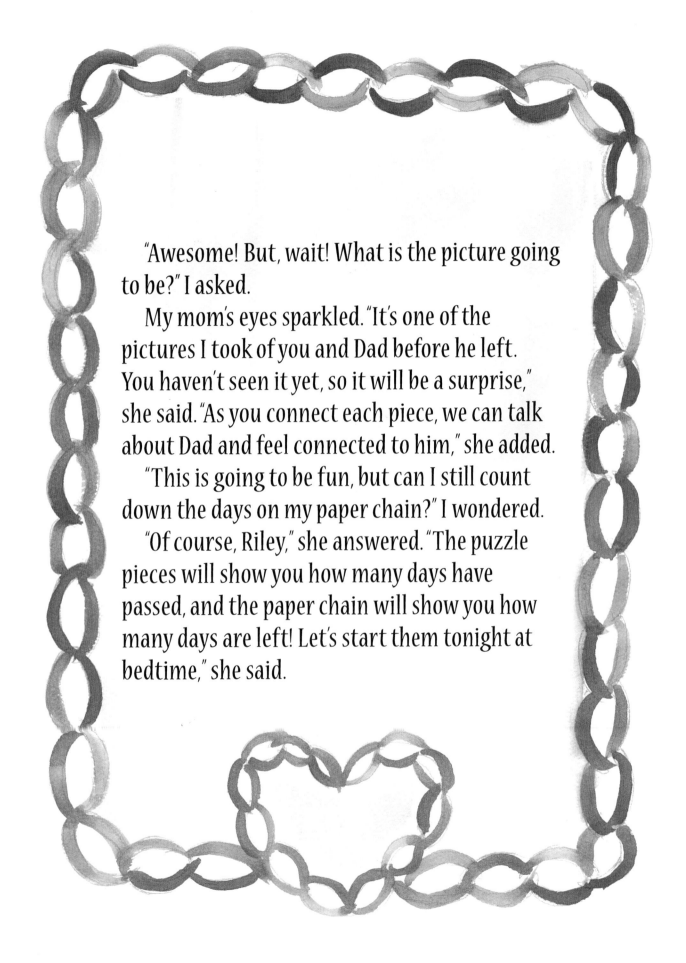

"Awesome! But, wait! What is the picture going to be?" I asked.

My mom's eyes sparkled. "It's one of the pictures I took of you and Dad before he left. You haven't seen it yet, so it will be a surprise," she said. "As you connect each piece, we can talk about Dad and feel connected to him," she added.

"This is going to be fun, but can I still count down the days on my paper chain?" I wondered.

"Of course, Riley," she answered. "The puzzle pieces will show you how many days have passed, and the paper chain will show you how many days are left! Let's start them tonight at bedtime," she said.

Later that night, as I was getting ready for bed, my mom came in my room and asked, "Are you ready for the count-DOWN, and the count-UP, to begin?"

"I sure am!" I cried. I tore the first link off my chain and then asked, "Where's the first piece of the puzzle?"

My mom smiled as she passed me the puzzle box. "In here. You have to find it. There's a number one on the back," she hinted.

It was sort of a game for me - it was fun, but a little tricky. While I searched for the piece with the number one written on the back, my mom and I talked about my dad. It was nice. She reminded me that there would be days when I would really miss him and that it was perfectly normal to cry about it. She also told me that I could talk to her about my feelings anytime and she would always try to make me feel better. I was glad about that!

"I found it!" I shouted. "The number one, the first piece!" I was excited until I flipped it over and saw that it was all blue.

"Hey! That's not fair! There's no clue about what the picture is going to be," I said.

My mom smiled again. "I guess the pieces are like days. Some are more exciting than others," she said. "But, each piece of the puzzle is important because it helps the puzzle grow; and each day is important because you learn things that help you grow bigger, smarter, and stronger."

"I have an idea," my mom continued. "Let's glue the pieces to this board so they'll stay connected and your puzzle won't fall apart. When it's done, we can frame it and hang it on your wall," she suggested.

"That would be cool!" I said.

Days went by, and sometimes I missed my dad a lot. I missed his hugs and I missed him tucking me in at night. Sometimes I was afraid he might forget about me, or that he'd forget about our secret handshake. But, he called us when he could, we emailed silly messages, and we even saw him on video chats a few times, too. It was good to see his face, but some days I missed him so much I cried.

We put one of my dad's sweatshirts on his chair at the kitchen table and we imagined him sitting with us at meals. Most of the time it was fun, but on the days when I missed my dad the most, seeing the sweatshirt there made me wish he was home even more.

On those extra sad days, my mom would give me extra hugs and say, "I miss Dad too, but each day we are closer to having him home again."

One day, my mom suggested we bake some cookies to send to my dad. We baked his favorites, and after we ate a few, we packed them in a box very carefully and filled the box with some of his

other favorite things from home. I drew him some pictures and my mom wrote him a letter. When my dad received the box, he was so happy and said he loved everything, especially my pictures!

Sometimes I was mad that my dad wasn't around and was missing all of the fun things that were happening, especially my birthday party. He didn't call me that day either. I was really mad at him! It just wasn't fair. Why did _my_ dad have to go away for so long? And, _how_ could he forget my birthday? Did he forget _me_ too?

That night, while I searched for the puzzle piece I needed, my mom and I talked about my dad like we always did. My mom explained that sailors can't make phone calls whenever they want; and it just happened to be a day my dad couldn't. She said he probably tried; and she was sure he thought about me all day.

I felt better after we talked, and when I stood back and looked at my puzzle, I could see it was turning out to be a picture of my dad hugging me! I could imagine how that hug felt. I closed my eyes and pretended it was real, just like my dad told me to. It felt good, and I knew he was doing the same thing when he looked at my pictures.

A few days after my party, a box came in the mail from my dad. There were some souvenirs and pictures from his last port visit and a birthday present for me! He _did_ remember me! And, he didn't forget my birthday either! I felt so much happier, and I loved all the surprises. They were awesome!

Later, he called to wish me a happy birthday and I told him all about my party. I was really glad he called!

Weeks went by, and we were busy. I played with friends, we explored new places, and we visited my grandparents. When we were busy, the time went by faster; and I realized that even though I missed my dad, there were so many things that made me happy. And, my mom was right. The days were like puzzle pieces – some were more exciting than others, and that's OK!

After a while, the paper chain was really short and my puzzle project was just about finished. My dad was almost home! My mom and I couldn't wait to see him again, and we talked about all of the things we wanted to do together as a family. I was especially excited to show him my puzzle project. I knew he would love it!

The last few days went by pretty fast. We had a lot to do to get ready for my dad to be home. We bought his favorite foods, cleaned the house, and made a big sign that said,

# "Welcome Home Dad!"

The big day finally arrived! My dad was coming home! My mom and I went to the pier where there were a lot of people holding signs just like ours. I was a little nervous, and I wondered if my dad would be any different, but I just couldn't wait to see him and have him home again. The ship finally pulled in and while the sailors were tying it to the pier, we spotted my dad on the deck. He saw us, too! Our eyes connected and it was *so awesome*!

Soon after that, I was running up to my dad and giving him the biggest, tightest, *squeeziest* hug I ever gave anyone! My mom joined us, and we all hugged for a long time. We were so happy to be together again and we couldn't stop smiling.

"How about that secret handshake, Riley? Do you remember it?" my dad asked.

"I sure do!" I answered. I was so relieved that <u>he</u> did too!

As we did our secret handshake, I felt my heart beating faster. I knew that even though my dad and I were apart, our hearts stayed connected. And, even though it wasn't easy to be apart, my family somehow grew a little stronger and closer with each day.

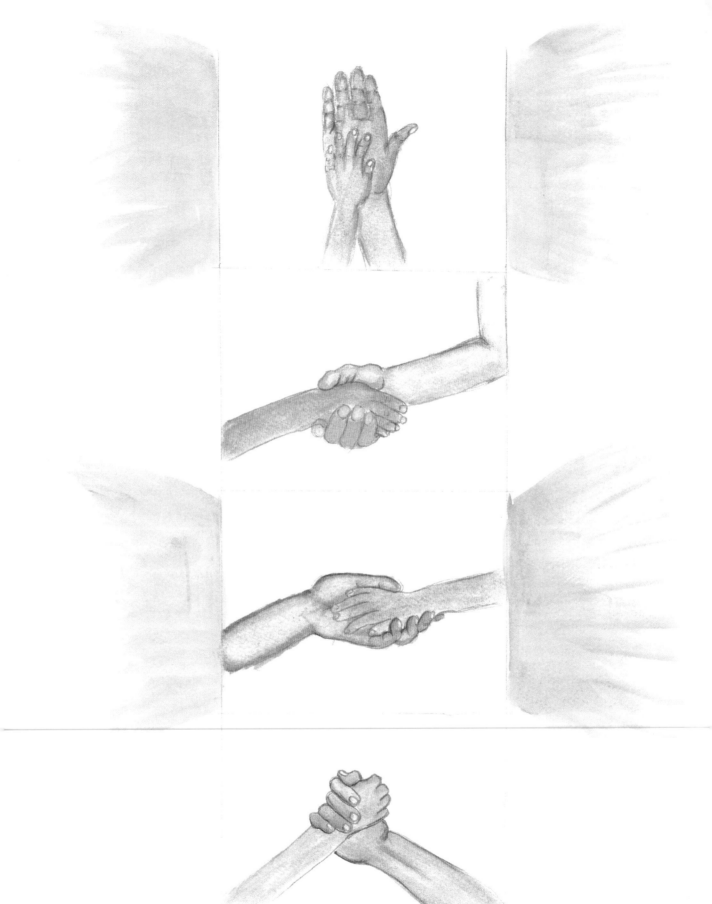

As soon as we got home, I showed my dad my puzzle project, and I let him glue the last piece of the puzzle to the board. Perfect! My puzzle project was complete and my super cool family was complete again too!

# Tips for your Puzzle Project
### based upon frequently asked questions

**Take a lot of pictures.**

❖ Most puzzle manufacturers require high resolution images for enlarging. Be careful if you crop your photo because it may negatively affect the resolution. Close-ups work best because you won't need to crop and there will be fewer background ("boring") puzzle pieces.

❖ Take several pictures in case one doesn't work as well as you'd like.

**Determine the number of pieces you need and the size of the puzzle you want.**

❖ The number of pieces you need is based on the number of days of the separation and how often you want to add pieces to your puzzle. Most puzzles come in standard sizes with a pre-set number of pieces (i.e. 110 pcs., 252 pcs.). I recommend ordering a puzzle with more pieces than you need because it will be easier to find ways to use extra pieces than it will be to skip days if you don't have enough. For example, if the separation is expected to be 180 days and your puzzle has 252 pieces, you can add more than one piece on certain days like birthdays, holidays, weekends, or "surprise bonus days" to make it more fun and to use the extra pieces. Also, since return dates often change, you might be glad to have some extra pieces.

❖ Research some puzzle manufacturing companies to find one that meets your puzzle needs and your budget. Check our website (see below*), or contact Donna Purkey at missyoutopieces@gmail.com for recommended links and more information.

**Allow time for processing.**

❖ Remember to allow time for processing, manufacturing, shipping, and your assembly (to write the numbers on the back). If it is not possible to have the puzzle ready on departure day, if the separation is <u>really</u> long, or even if the return date is too variable, you can always start the puzzle at a point during the deployment (i.e. the half-way point).

**Prepare and Assemble**.

❖ When your puzzle arrives, let the fun begin! Assemble it yourself and number the backs of the puzzle pieces in order. I recommend starting at the top left corner and numbering across the top row. Continue across each row, finishing at the bottom right.

❖ Keep the puzzle pieces safe in the original box or in a zippered bag when you are not working on your puzzle. If your children are very young, you may want to separate the pieces into smaller groups (of 10, 25 or 50) for them to find the pieces more easily. Searching for the pieces is an excellent way to develop those fine motor skills and will help your young children learn how to count!

❖ Choose a time of day to work on the puzzle. Making it part of the bedtime routine works well. Be consistent so your children will look forward to it and will know they have the chance each day/night to talk to you about their feelings, their day, their deployed parent, etc. Make it an opportunity to connect. Share your thoughts and feelings (as appropriate) with them and talk to them about your day as well.

❖ Choose an area to work on your puzzle. Remember, you will be working on it for months! I recommend using a glue stick or a very small dot of liquid glue to adhere the pieces onto a poster board or foam board each day. This allows the puzzle to be more portable (and of course, will keep the puzzle together - the last thing you want is to have it fall apart!).

**Additional Comments**:

❖ If you have more than one child, decide ahead of time if they will each have their own puzzle, if they will each add a piece a day, or if they will alternate who adds the piece. This will influence the number of pieces you need and your choice of photograph as well!

❖ Try not to intentionally skip days unless you can come up with a good "excuse" to do so. Your children are most likely looking forward to that part of their day and will be disappointed if it's skipped. Furthermore, never punish your children by not allowing them to add their daily piece because of a behavioral issue or something that happened during the day. Working on the puzzle should always be a <u>positive</u> experience.

❖ It is up to you, based on your children, if you want to show them what the puzzle picture is going to be or if you are going to leave it a surprise. It is fun either way!

❖ Be inspired, be creative, and nurture the bonds between your children and their loved ones.

*website at time of publishing is
www.missyoutopieces.com and is subject to change.

Feel free to contact the author, Donna Purkey, at missyoutopieces@gmail.com

Made in the USA
Charleston, SC
12 October 2012